PERFORMANCE-ENHANCING
DRUGS IN SPORTS

BY TONY KHING

Published by ABDO Publishing Company, PO Box 398166, Minneapolis, MN 55439. Copyright © 2014 by Abdo Consulting Group, Inc. International copyrights reserved in all countries. No part of this book may be reproduced in any form without written permission from the publisher. SportsZone™ is a trademark and logo of ABDO Publishing Company.

Printed in the United States of America,
North Mankato, Minnesota
102013
012014

♻ THIS BOOK CONTAINS AT LEAST 10% RECYCLED MATERIALS.

Editor: Chrös McDougall
Series Designer: Craig Hinton

Photo credits: Pavel L Photo and Video/Shutterstock Images, cover, 1; Franck Faugere/DPPI/Icon SMI, 5; Jeff Roberson/AP Images, 9; Manuel Balce Ceneta/AP Images, 13; Wolfgang Rattay/Reuters/ Corbis, 15; Winai Tepsuttinun/Shutterstock Images, 17; Joe Belanger/Shutterstock Images, 21; Marcio Jose Sanchez/AP Images, 27; Jae C. Hong/AP Images, 29; The State, Charles Slate/AP Images, 31; Mel Evans/AP Images, 35; Bebeto Matthews/AP Images, 39; Kevork Djansezian/AP Images, 41; Jason DeCrow/AP Images, 43; Al Behrman/AP Images, 46; Bettmann/Corbis, 49; Rick Rycroft/AP Images, 51; Kathy Willens/AP Images, 54; Alex Teh/AP Images, 59

Library of Congress Control Number: 2013946562

Cataloging-in-Publication Data

Khing, Tony.
 Performance-enhancing drugs in sports / Tony Khing.
    p. cm. -- (Issues in sports)
Includes bibliographical references and index.
ISBN 978-1-62403-124-3
1. Doping in sports--Juvenile literature. 2. Steroids--Juvenile literature. 3. Anabolic steroids-- Juvenile literature. I. Title.
362.29--dc23

                                                            2013946562

Content Consultant: James E. Leone, PhD, MS, LAT, ATC, CSCS, *D, CHES, FMHI
Associate Professor of Health at Bridgewater State University

TABLE OF CONTENTS

CHAPTER 1

DOPING MATTERS

Everyone loves a winner. One person who knew that well was Lance Armstrong. He was always a competitive athlete. In his teens, Armstrong was a talented triathlete. Then he switched to cycling. As a cyclist, Armstrong did things no one had done before.

The Tour de France is the world's most famous bike race. It is a grueling test of speed and endurance. Cyclists race upwards of 2,000 miles (3,219 km). The race lasts approximately three weeks. Many stages are more than 100 miles (161 km). Some stages require cyclists to ride up mountains. Just completing the race is considered an achievement.

From 1999 to 2005, Armstrong won all seven Tours. And he began his streak just three years after being diagnosed with testicular cancer.

Armstrong became an icon in the United States during this run. He had overcome cancer. He was a leading advocate for cancer awareness. He was historically successful in one of the world's most difficult sporting events. On top of all that, Armstrong was believed to be one of the clean riders of his era.

Cycling has a long history of doping. Doping is when athletes use illegal substances, or performance-enhancing drugs (PEDs), to gain a competitive advantage. Many top riders from Armstrong's era were later found to be using PEDs. All sports have different rules for what is and is not allowed. The punishments for being caught using PEDs differ depending on the sport. Regardless of the sport, however, PEDs are shunned in sports. Athletes who use PEDs are labeled as cheaters. Plus, research has shown that PED use can be harmful to one's health. Using a banned substance to improve in sports is a huge risk.

Armstrong was aggressive in telling fans that he was winning without PEDs.

////////////

DOPING

PEDs come in all different types. Some drugs help athletes develop bigger muscles. Some drugs improve endurance. Other drugs help by giving a person more energy or by limiting anxiety. Whether or not an athlete is allowed to use the substances depends on the sport. Each sport has different rules and a different list of banned substances. The general term to describe the use of banned substances is "doping." The term originated sometime in the 1900s. However, the word likely comes from the word *dop*. Dop was an alcoholic beverage Zulu soldiers of Africa used to drink before battle. It helped them perform better.

//

He strongly denied any accusations of doping. After all, Armstrong would point out, he never officially failed a drug test. That helped him build an image as one of the few clean riders in a sport full of cheaters.

Some people had their doubts about Armstrong, though. They knew about the history of doping in cycling. They knew that many top riders in Armstrong's era were linked to PEDs. And they knew that Armstrong's results were too good to be true.

Armstrong angrily denied these accusations. He even went as far as to sue those who claimed to have evidence that he was doping. Eventually the evidence piled up, though. Journalists dug deeper into his background. The US government opened an investigation. Former friends and teammates came out saying Armstrong had doped. Soon the US Anti-Doping Agency (USADA) got involved. USADA concluded in 2012 that Armstrong had used PEDs. Armstrong's world was crashing down. Finally, in January 2013, he came clean. Armstrong was no longer a winner; he was a cheater.

"I'm a flawed character," Armstrong said when he admitted his actions. "I viewed this situation as one big lie that I repeated a lot of times."

NOT THE FIRST

Armstrong's fall from grace was swift and dramatic. Some people stood by him because of his support of cancer awareness. But to most, Armstrong went from a national hero to a fraud. The International Cycling Union (UCI) wiped away all of his victories. Companies that had stood by him ended their relationships. Armstrong was even forced to step down as chairman of his own cancer-fighting charity, Livestrong.

Armstrong's story showed the two sides to doping. PEDs helped him achieve sports success. That success in turn helped him become rich and famous. But the PEDs also took away that success, that popularity, and much of his money when he came clean. How those PEDs will affect his long-term health is yet to be seen.

Armstrong was hardly the first athlete to use PEDs. And he wasn't the first athlete to be caught either. Athletes in a wide range of sports have been caught using PEDs. And the users range from superstars to scrubs. They all have different reasons.

Some athletes see PEDs as the only option. The difference between making a pro team and not making a pro team can be slim. In some cases, PEDs have put an athlete over the edge. Sometimes athletes feel pressure to keep up. This is especially true in sports where other athletes are known to be using. Other times athletes view PEDs as a path to stardom. The rewards of athletic success—such as big paychecks and fame—are powerful motivators. Sometimes PEDs can help speed up recovery from an injury.

No matter what the reason, PEDs can have serious and long-term effects on one's health, social life, public standing, and well-being. And the effects are often felt by more than just the user.

Milwaukee Brewers outfielder Ryan Braun ▲
connects for a hit during the 2011 playoffs. He
was later accused of doping during that season.

STOLEN GLORY

Milwaukee Brewers outfielder Ryan Braun was on fire in 2011. He had a
.332 batting average while hitting 33 home runs and driving in 111 runs.
The Brewers' 96 wins were the most in team history. And after the season,
Braun was named the National League (NL) Most Valuable Player (MVP).

Before long, however, Braun was linked to PEDs. At first, he denied
that he had doped. Then, in 2013, he came clean. Braun had been injured

in 2011. He said he had used illegal substances to help speed up his recovery. Major League Baseball (MLB) banned Braun for 65 games.

Losing Braun for 65 games hurt the Brewers. Braun's doping hurt others, too. Los Angeles Dodgers outfielder Matt Kemp also had a great season in 2011. He finished second to Braun in the NL MVP voting. After Braun's suspension, Kemp said he felt "betrayed." Kemp also said the MVP Award should be given to him. Winning the award could have helped Kemp earn more money from his team and from sponsors.

Similar stories happen on a smaller level too. A 2012 *Sports Illustrated* report looked back at four pitchers. All four played on the same minor league team in 1994. All four were right-handed, were around the same age, and had similar abilities. But only one of those players made the major leagues. And that player was the only one who used PEDs. Brett Roberts was one of the players who did not make it. He learned of his former teammate's PED use while watching a television interview several years later.

"I was very upset, knowing my chance to get to the big leagues was cut short," Roberts said. "I was jealous, hurt, frustrated, angry . . . all that stuff."

HEALTH PROBLEMS

Lyle Alzado was a star professional football player. He played in the National Football League (NFL) for 15 years. Alzado even won a Super

Bowl with the Los Angeles Raiders. And he was using anabolic steroids the whole time.

"I never stopped," he said. "Not when I retired from the NFL in 1985. Not ever."

Alzado started taking anabolic steroids for one reason. "I was so wild about winning," he said. "It's all I cared about—winning, winning. I never talked about anything else." Alzado said that the PEDs made him "play better and better." He kept taking the drugs because he had to get bigger physically to play at his best.

Alzado was getting better on the field, but he was different off of it. "People say steroids can make you mean and moody," Alzado said. "My mood swings were incredible." He admitted to doing things "only crazy people do."

Six years after retiring from football, in 1991, Alzado was diagnosed with brain cancer. He died one year later. Anabolic steroids cause many negative health problems. Doctors have never established a link between PEDs and brain cancer. But Alzado believed anabolic steroids caused his

////////////////////////////

MARK McGWIRE

MLB was struggling to get fans interested after a work stoppage in 1994. Then Mark McGwire and Sammy Sosa came along. They spent the summer of 1998 chasing baseball's single-season home run record. Both players surpassed the previous record of 61. McGwire, the St. Louis Cardinals' first baseman, ended the season with 70. The home run chase sparked great interest in baseball. But today it is no longer celebrated. In 2010, McGwire admitted that he used PEDs during the 1998 season. Sosa has long been linked to PEDs as well. They were once shoo-ins to make the Hall of Fame. That fate is no longer certain. "I'm certainly sorry for having done it," McGwire said. "It's the most regrettable thing I've ever done in my life."

////////////////////////////

cancer. He went public with his story before his death. Alzado told others not to follow his example by using anabolic steroids.

FALLING FROM GRACE

In the United States, MLB has been at the center of the PEDs discussion. The sport saw a major rise in power hitting during the 1990s. At first fans loved it. Then they became wary. They realized that the power hitting was unnatural. But baseball had no anti-doping policy at the time. It became clear to those in and around the league that changes needed to take place.

Congress got involved to investigate. The investigation's results were released in the 2007 Mitchell Report. The report claimed that dozens of players were using PEDs. Among the players were some of the biggest stars from the 1990s and early 2000s.

Pitcher Roger Clemens dominated the majors for 24 seasons. He won more than 350 games and struck out more than 4,600 batters. Plus, he won seven Cy Young Awards from 1986 to 2004. That award is given to the best pitcher in each league each season. He was one of the best ever. Then his name showed up in the Mitchell Report.

Clemens has denied ever using PEDs. In 2008, Clemens even told Congress that he had competed clean. But government officials did not believe him. It is illegal to lie to federal officials. The government took Clemens to court. He was eventually acquitted in 2012. Still, it is widely believed that Clemens used PEDs.

Clemens retired after the 2007 season. In 2013, he was eligible for the National Baseball Hall of Fame. At least 75 percent of voters needed to select him in order for him to get in. A first-ballot selection would have been expected a few years earlier. In 2013, Clemens only received 37.6 percent of the votes.

That does not mean Clemens is out forever. The voters elect new members every year. But many people believe players linked to PEDs should never get in. Hall of Fame pitcher Goose Gossage is among those who agree.

"It's like telling our kids you can cheat, you can do whatever you want, and it's not going to matter," Gossage said.

THE BATTLE TO PREVENT DOPING

PEDs have been an issue in sports for decades. Doping in athletic competitions goes back even further. The battle to combat doping is relatively young, though. Sports began banning PEDs in the early 1900s. Testing became more common in the 1960s and 1970s. But high-profile doping scandals still rocked sports in the 1980s and 1990s.

Athletes in sports such as baseball, cycling, and track and field were increasingly found to be using PEDs. This put those sports' integrity into question. The athletes were at risk of health problems. Sometimes athletes had to forfeit wins after testing positive for drugs. In baseball, athletes using PEDs broke cherished records. Ultimately, athletes, fans, and sponsors felt cheated. They wondered why they should invest time or money into a sport where some competitors had an unfair advantage. Sports leagues were forced to step up and address the problem.

A LOSING BATTLE?

Some people see testing for PEDs as a losing battle. The tests might catch some users, they say. However, the PEDs usually evolve faster than the tests. That means some users might never be caught. That is what happened with Lance Armstrong. He used PEDs that could not be traced. Or he found other ways to avoid drug tests. With legal doping, all athletes could have the same advantage. In addition, some people argue that athletes should have control over their own bodies. If they want to risk future medical problems, that is their choice. The overwhelming approach in sports has been to limit doping, however. Sports organizations do not want a system where athletes feel like they must use PEDs to be competitive.

Cyclist Lance Armstrong rose to the top of his sport by doping, but doping wiped away all of his victories and resulted in fans turning on him.

The battle against doping is international and sophisticated. Athletes in many sports are tested regularly. Scientists are constantly working on new tests. But still, doping persists. So sports officials, doctors, athletes, and fans continue to work to find new solutions to stop one of the oldest problems in sports.

CHAPTER 2

Sports officials view doping as a major threat to both athlete health and sports integrity. ▶

PED BASICS

A performance-enhancing drug is any substance that gives an athlete an unfair edge over the competition. But there is no universal definition of what is fair and unfair. Each sports organization has its own list of fair and unfair substances. And each sports organization has its own approach to detecting and punishing PED users.

Doping has existed as far back as the ancient Greek Olympics. Meat was not a normal part of the diet in ancient Greece. But athletes in the ancient Greek Olympics are believed to have feasted on meat. They believed eating meat would make their muscles stronger for the competition.

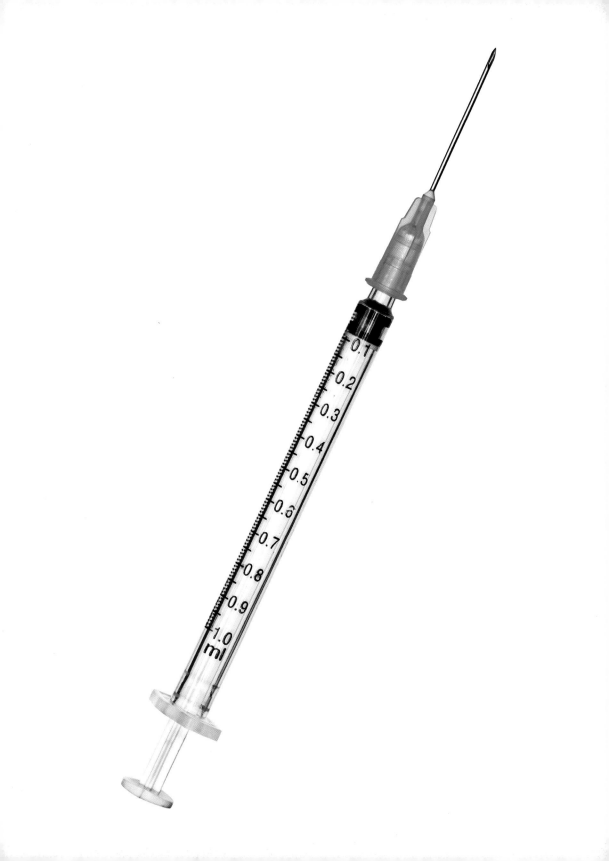

Modern doping developed alongside modern sports. Many of today's most popular sports were founded during the 1800s. Professional leagues and other competitions formed around that time. During the 1900s, these sports grew into major operations. Success in sports could mean great fame or a big paycheck. Those perks in turn created more motivation to be successful at all costs.

Early doping methods were less sophisticated. Athletes were found to have used alcohol and crude stimulants to boost their performance. Then anabolic steroids were introduced in the 1950s. That began a revolution in doping. PEDs developed into a big business. Scientists worked to find new substances that could help an athlete improve. Sports officials worked to identify and ban those substances. Then scientists found ways to avoid detection. Or the scientists simply found new substances. That is the complex world in which sports doping exists today.

CREATINE

Dietary supplements are usually legal in sports and daily life. That is because their results are achievable through natural means. One of the most common supplements is creatine. Creatine is produced naturally by the human body and found in the muscles. Scientists can also make a man-made version. Not all athletes respond to creatine. But studies have shown that creatine can improve athletic performance and increase muscle mass. It is likely safe when used properly. But high doses of creatine could be unsafe. Creatine can cause muscle cramping and stomach pain. Some medical professionals believe creatine could affect the function of the kidneys, liver, and heart. Creatine use will result in weight gain because it helps hold water in the muscles. However, most sports organizations allow athletes to use creatine.

Technically, any substance can affect one's athletic performance. For example, a balanced diet can make one's body function better. But no sports organizations regulate an athlete's basic diet. In sports, PEDs usually refer to substances that can have potent effects on one's body. Sometimes these are illegal substances such as man-made hormones. Sometimes the substances are only legal when prescribed by a doctor for medical reasons. And other times PEDs are substances such as dietary supplements that are legally sold in stores. On many occasions, a substance is fair in one sport but banned in another.

Each sports organization has its own criteria for fair and unfair, safe and unsafe. Many sports follow the lead of the World Anti-Doping Agency (WADA). WADA sets anti-doping standards for all of the Olympic sports. It considers fairness, health, and equality in making its guidelines.

ANABOLIC STEROIDS

By far the most common PEDs are anabolic steroids. These exist in various forms. In fact, doctors prescribe some types of steroids for legitimate medical purposes. But anabolic steroids artificially enhance bodily function. They also put users at risk of serious health problems. As such, all forms of anabolic steroids are banned in the Olympic Games and the major US sports leagues.

Anabolic steroids are a man-made form of testosterone. Testosterone is the male sex hormone. Among other things, it triggers the development of male sex characteristics. However, anabolic steroids also promote cell growth. That means they can aid muscle growth and recovery. The latter effect is what makes anabolic steroids appealing to many athletes.

"You can train as hard as you can," said Mimi D'Attomo, a former female bodybuilder. "But realistically, it's almost impossible to make gains without [anabolic steroids], because [anabolic steroids] help you recuperate so you never really feel the aches and pains."

The first known use of steroids in sports came in 1952. Weightlifters from the Soviet Union used testosterone to improve their performance. The next step was anabolic steroids. US doctor John Ziegler developed these after the 1956 Olympics. He promoted the steroids to help the US Olympic weightlifting team with muscle growth and performance.

Anabolic steroid use became increasingly popular during the late 1960s and the 1970s. Some sports organizations moved to try to eliminate anabolic steroids from sports. The first test was developed in 1974. The first Olympic Games in which anabolic steroids were banned was in 1976. But these tests and bans proved to be lacking. Athletes still found ways to get around the tests. Plus, the efforts to combat anabolic steroid use were largely limited to Olympic sports.

Tests have improved significantly over the years. However, athletes still use anabolic steroids more than any other PED. In 2012, WADA reported that 50.6 percent of all doping violations involved anabolic steroids. That number was more than three times as high as any other category of PEDs. It shows that many athletes still believe they can get away with using anabolic steroids. They see the potential reward as greater than the risk of being caught.

However, anabolic steroids have serious health risks. In men, the effects can include developing breasts and shrunken testicles. Women might grow more body hair, develop a deeper voice, and have issues with menstruation. Both men and women can develop serious acne and baldness from anabolic steroids as well. In addition, anabolic steroid use might change one's personality. Users might become moody or quick tempered. They also may become more likely to be physically violent when they become angry. These personality changes are sometimes referred to as "roid rage."

Anabolic steroid use can also result in more serious, long-term health problems. People who use them for a long time are likely to have higher blood pressure. That means the heart must work harder than normal to pump blood through the body. Long-term high blood pressure puts more stress on the body. That could decrease the length of one's life. Anabolic steroids can also raise a user's cholesterol levels. Too much cholesterol can prevent blood from properly flowing into the heart and through the body. Anabolic steroids can also damage the liver.

OTHER PEDS

Although all sports have different standards for what PEDs are banned, many follow WADA's guidelines either exactly or closely, including banning masking agents. Here are some other common types of banned PEDs:

OTHER ANABOLIC AGENTS: Anabolic steroids are man-made testosterone that can help build muscles. Scientists have developed other man-made hormones that can have similar effects. These building substances are all called anabolic agents.

Androstenedione, or andro, is one example. This hormone is released naturally in the body. When released, it is converted to testosterone. The PED form mimics the effects of testosterone. It is said that andro helps athletes build muscle faster and speed recovery after a hard workout. Scientists disagree as to whether andro actually works. However, the substance is illegal in the United States unless prescribed by a doctor.

Andro has negative side effects. It can cause people to take on physical traits of the opposite sex. These traits can include developing breasts in men and baldness in women.

Human growth hormone (HGH) is also used as a PED. The hormone releases naturally from people's brains throughout their lifetimes. It helps the body grow and maintain tissues. Some people are prescribed human-made HGH for medical reasons. As a PED, some believe it has similar effects to anabolic steroids. However, doctors dispute if it actually works. What is known is that HGH can cause negative side effects. These can include joint and muscle pain, as well as heart disease and diabetes.

EPO: Erythropoietin, or EPO, is a naturally occurring hormone. This hormone is naturally released when a person has low levels of oxygen in the blood. However, athletes use EPO to unnaturally increase oxygen levels in their blood. Increased oxygen allows muscles to be more effective and recover faster. Because of that, EPO is most commonly used by endurance athletes. However, EPO can have dangerous effects on people's blood. The blood of an EPO user becomes thicker. So athletes who use EPO are at a higher risk for heart attacks and strokes. As a result, EPO can be deadly. EPO is one of the PEDs Armstrong admitted to using.

WORLD ANTI-DOPING CODE

In 2004, WADA introduced the World Anti-Doping Code. The code is like the constitution of anti-doping. It outlines the policies, rules, and regulations for doping. The code includes a list of banned substances. It also standardizes approaches for testing, labs, exemptions, and privacy. The code has been credited with simplifying and standardizing doping regulations. The code was updated in 2009.

BLOOD DOPING

Some athletes use illegal techniques to increase their number of red blood cells. This is called blood doping. The idea is that more red blood cells result in more oxygen in the muscles. That helps one's muscles work harder and longer. As such, blood doping is particularly common in endurance sports such as cycling. EPO is one form of blood doping. Another way athletes increase red blood cells is through blood transfusions. This is where blood is taken from a rested athlete and stored. Later the oxygen-rich blood is put into a tired athlete's body. This is banned in most sports and can result in several serious side effects, such as a heart attack or stroke. A third type of blood doping is through synthetic oxygen carriers. These are man-made proteins or chemicals that carry oxygen. However, this also comes with serious health risks.

STIMULANTS: The second-most common PEDs are stimulants. These are substances that improve an athlete's focus and energy. Stimulants can be found in many substances. The caffeine in coffee, for example, is a stimulant. Mild stimulants such as coffee and energy drinks are allowed in sports. Sports governing bodies are more concerned with stimulants such as amphetamines. Amphetamines are normally used to treat conditions such as hyperactivity. But taken without supervision or for sports, they can be dangerous. Stimulants increase one's heart rate and blood pressure. The drugs can lead to problems with anxiety, insomnia, or even heart attacks and strokes.

In 2013, MLB star Miguel Tejada tested positive for an amphetamine called Adderall. Doctors prescribe Adderall to help people with attention deficit hyperactivity disorder (ADHD). Tejada has ADHD. However, he did not have MLB clearance to use the drug. The positive test for a banned substance resulted in a 105-game suspension.

PAINKILLERS: Many painkillers are widely available for public purchase. Painkillers are not necessarily harmful, either. People and athletes regularly use them to manage everyday aches and pains. Sports officials must weigh if masking pain in competition is a form of unfair performance enhancing.

"In my opinion painkillers fulfill all requirements of a doping substance because normally pain is a protection mechanism of the body and with painkillers you switch off this protection system, like if you switch off fatigue, which is also a protection mechanism of the body," said Dr. Hans Geyer, who works at a doping lab in Germany.

Simple painkillers such as aspirin are allowed in sports. The strongest painkillers are only available with a prescription. The focus for many organizations is promoting safe use of these drugs. Some people become addicted to painkillers. Also, pain is a natural signal from the body. Sometimes people using painkillers think they are healthier than they are. This can lead to serious injuries.

DIURETICS: Diuretics do not improve one's performance. However, they are a masking agent. That means they hide other PEDs in the body. Because of this, diuretics, such as plasma expanders, are banned in most sports. WADA bans diuretics.

Diuretics work by decreasing the amount of salt and water in one's body. When prescribed by a doctor, these drugs can treat high blood pressure and other health problems. However, athletes usually use diuretics because they dilute urine. This hides other drugs in one's body. Athletes also sometimes misuse diuretics to lose weight. This is common in sports such as wrestling where athletes compete in weight classes.

The side effects from diuretics can be extreme. They include dehydration, dizziness, and low blood pressure. Misuse of diuretics can also be fatal.

GLUCOCORTICOSTEROIDS: Glucocorticosteroids reduce inflammation. As hormones, they occur naturally in the body. They are used regularly in medicine, such as inhaled asthma treatment. But glucocorticosteroids can cause long-term harm when used improperly. These substances can harm the joints, muscles, bones, tendons, and ligaments.

Glucocorticosteroids might be PEDs depending on how they are used. WADA bans all use of glucocorticosteroids. Other sports allow the drugs in certain conditions, such as when athletes are not in season. And some glucocorticosteroids are allowed. Many baseball players rely on cortisone shots throughout the long season. Cortisone reduces inflammation. This helps athletes quickly mask pain so they can continue playing. Despite masking the pain, cortisone does not help one's body heal. That makes it potentially dangerous. An athlete with a cortisone shot can worsen damage to an already injured joint, ligament, or tendon.

BETA-BLOCKERS: Beta-blockers lower one's blood pressure by limiting the amount of adrenaline his or her body can produce. Outside of sports, people commonly and legally use beta-blockers to treat heart conditions

Not all PEDs help an athlete become stronger. ▲
Beta-blockers help athletes such as golfers and
archers by reducing nerves and anxiety.

or to manage blood pressure. However, beta-blockers can calm the nerves
and reduce anxiety. They also limit muscle spasms. This can be an unfair
advantage, especially in sports such as archery or golf. Beta-blockers
can also be dangerous if used for nonmedical reasons. Most sports
organizations ban beta-blockers.

"In my day, lots of guys were on beta blockers," said golfer Greg
Norman, who starred during the 1980s and 1990s. "It wasn't openly
acknowledged, but it was obvious to the rest of us. A guy's personality
would change. In practice rounds or friendly matches, we'd see the real

guy under stress. Then in competition, he was like a different, calmer person. Those guys were trying to take the nerves out of the game. But nerves are very much a part of the game."

CANNABINOIDS: Most people think of marijuana as a street drug, not a PED. But most sports leagues ban the drug nonetheless. That is in part because marijuana is illegal in most countries. In addition, marijuana can impair one's mental state. This can be dangerous in sports to both the athlete and others. However, there is a movement to loosen penalties for cannabinoids. These people argue that marijuana is safe and does not enhance one's performance like other PEDs.

////////////////////////

GENE DOPING

According to WADA's Web site, gene doping "represents a threat to the integrity of sport and the health of athletes." That is why the organization is trying to get ahead of the trend before it begins. Gene doping is when athletes modify their genes to get a competitive advantage. It is similar to gene therapy, a legal medical process already being used. But gene doping could have serious health risks, including cancer. WADA bans any gene doping. However, WADA announced in June 2013 that it was still working on a reliable detection test. "There seems to be mental readiness to [try gene doping] once it is available in some sort of safe way," a WADA official said.

////////////////////////////////

DETECTION NOT SO SIMPLE

PEDs come in many different forms. Identifying them is not always straightforward. Banned substances might appear in a product that otherwise seems harmless. As such, many athletes who have positive tests say they did not mean to use a banned substance.

Many top athletes use products to help their performance. Athletes are encouraged to always consult with team doctors or other experts before using the products.

Scientists work at a doping control laboratory at ▲ the 2010 Olympic Winter Games in Vancouver.

Sports organizations have lists of banned substances available. So even if an athlete uses a PED by accident, the athlete is held at fault.

The science of doping is constantly changing as well. Some doctors and scientists are constantly working to develop new PEDs. Other doctors and scientists are constantly studying those new PEDs. These doctors create tests so that bans can be enforced. However, a test can only go into effect after a new PED is discovered. That means that athletes are usually ahead of the testers. The anti-doping scientists are catching up, though. And punishments for those caught are getting steeper and steeper.

CHAPTER 3

PED use is growing in the lower levels of sports, too. ▶
Andre Rienzo, a minor league baseball player, was
suspended for using PEDs in 2012.

DOPING AT LOWER LEVELS

PEDs are a visible problem in the top levels of sports. Those athletes are in the spotlight. Sometimes they make a lot of money. When caught, they are labeled "cheats" and blamed for ruining the integrity of the game.

Experts are increasingly concerned with what happens outside the spotlight. They are finding that PED use is spreading to the amateur levels of sports. Youth and high school sports are more competitive than they used to be. More and more kids are seeking a competitive edge by using banned substances. These kids see professional athletes using PEDs and think it is an acceptable practice. But youth and amateur athletes

BODYBUILDING

Some athletes use anabolic steroids to increase their performance in sports. Another reason people use these PEDs is to look better. The sport of bodybuilding is all about physically developing one's muscles. Competitive bodybuilders are judged based on their appearance. Anti-doping measures are lax for elite bodybuilders. That has led to extensive anabolic steroid use within the sport. Additionally, many companies advertise supplements or other drugs specifically to bodybuilders. These substances are usually legal over the counter. However, oftentimes they are not allowed by WADA and other sports organizations. Doctors warn that people should research these substances carefully before using them.

face unique challenges with doping. Their battles with the mental and physical side effects of PEDs often take place away from the public eye.

Taylor Hooton had everything going for him. He was a popular 17-year-old at his high school in Texas. And he was going to be the ace pitcher on the baseball team in his senior year. But Hooton was not happy. He did not like himself. He wanted to be bigger.

A high school baseball coach suggested Hooton should get bigger, too. So Hooton started taking anabolic steroids. He gained 30 pounds (13.6 kg). He looked bigger. But his personality changed, too. He would get very angry frequently. Hooton even threw a phone through a wall.

Hooton eventually admitted to using anabolic steroids and stopped using the drugs. Shortly after, he went on a family vacation. But while on vacation, he stole a camera and a laptop computer. That was out of character for him. Then, a day later, Hooton killed himself. Doctors believed Hooton's death came from the mental effects of stopping anabolic steroid use. Dr. Larry Gibbons, a medical director of a top preventive medicine clinic in Dallas, said:

> It's a pretty strong case that [Hooton] was withdrawing from steroids and his suicide was directly related to that. . . . This is a kid who was well liked, had a lot of good friends, no serious emotional problems. He had a bright future.

PEDS IN YOUTH SPORTS: MANY UNKNOWNS

Hooton was hardly alone as a high school PED user. Researchers studied 2,800 youths throughout the Minneapolis-St. Paul metro area during the 2009–10 school year. The study found that 5 percent of these high school and middle school students had used anabolic steroids. Approximately 5–10 percent of these youths used other substances, such as creatine, to build muscles. Meanwhile, approximately 33 percent of boys and 20 percent of girls had used protein powders or similar supplements.

Other studies have shown similar results. It is believed approximately a half-million high school students in the United States have used PEDs. Researchers have found that PED use is more common in boys than in girls. And the users tend to be athletes in power sports, such as football, baseball, weightlifting, and gymnastics.

Doping in youth sports brings up questions of fairness and integrity. However, doctors are most concerned with the effects PEDs can have on young bodies. Youths who use PEDs are at risk of the same side effects experienced by adults. Some issues are unique to young people, though. For example, kids who use PEDs might experience stunted growth.

Yet most concerning to doctors is what they don't know. Studies have been done on the long-term effects of anabolic steroids and other PEDs on adults. But there has been little study on long-term effects among youth users. Researchers have focused more seriously on this trend in recent years.

"We used to be concerned that the athletes were using [PEDs] at the elite level, the professionals, the aspiring Olympians," said Dr. David Marshall of the University of Michigan Health System. "But now we are starting to find that these types of performance-enhancing substances are coming down more to the high school levels, and recent studies show that the junior high kids are also starting to get involved in banned, illegal performance-enhancing substances, and that is concerning us."

Another consideration is that most PEDs are not commercially available. Doctors can prescribe some steroids and other PEDs for legitimate medical reasons. But most of the PEDs used by athletes come from the black market. That means there is no government oversight of the manufacturers or distributors.

"You never know what's really inside, in terms of components," said Dr. Anne Moore, who specializes in sports medicine. "Are they tainted? There certainly have been reports of people that have been using steroids

As high school sports become more and more ▲ competitive, young athletes are feeling more temptation to use PEDs to bulk up.

and other kinds of injectable medications and things like that that have been tainted with other chemicals."

A GROWING PROBLEM

There are many reasons youth athletes might use PEDs. Many young people are insecure about their bodies. They might begin using PEDs in order to put on weight or get bigger muscles. Youth and high school

The Mayo Clinic in Rochester, Minnesota, is one of the world's most esteemed hospitals and medical research institutions. Experts have posted several articles about PEDs on the clinic's Web site. One article discusses the risks of PED use among teens. It lists five "red flags" that might identify a PED user.

▶ Behavioral, emotional, or psychological changes—particularly increased aggressiveness ("roid rage")

▶ Changes in body build, including muscle growth, rapid weight gain, and development of the upper body

▶ Increased acne and facial bloating

▶ Needle marks in the buttocks or thighs

▶ Enlarged breasts in boys or smaller breasts in girls

> Source: Mayo Clinic Staff. "Performance-enhancing drugs and teen athletes." Mayo Clinic. Mayo Foundation for Medical Education and Research, 22 Aug. 2013. Web. 7 Sept. 2013.

Changing Minds

Pretend that a friend or a teammate is showing some of the "red flags" listed above. In addition, that friend is also performing really well on the playing field. How would you approach the situation? What evidence from this chapter can you use to help convince the friend that PED use is harmful?

sports are also becoming more intense. That was the case in Hooton's hometown of Plano, Texas. He felt great pressure to succeed for his school. Many athletes also see PEDs as a way to help earn an athletic scholarship or reach a professional career.

Youth sports are only a short part of people's lives. Only 2 percent of youth athletes earn athletic scholarships. The number of kids who go on to make a living as an athlete is even lower. Yet more and more kids are risking their health to improve their sports careers.

Also concerning is that kids sometimes feel pressured to use. Hooton's parents initially had no idea their son was using anabolic steroids. Once they found out, they tried to get him to stop. The *Sun Sentinel* newspaper in Florida investigated PEDs in 2013. It found that some parents actually encourage their young athletes to use PEDs.

"The parents hear that these things are possibly available, and that pro athletes are using them, and they want to know if that's something their son or daughter—usually son—can use for competitive advantage," Dr. Ernesto Blanco, a pediatric endocrinologist, told the *Sun Sentinel*.

GETTING DOPING OUT OF YOUTH SPORTS

Most professional sports leagues have drug tests and anti-doping policies for top-level athletes. Testing for high school, youth, and amateur athletes is not common, though. There are different reasons for this. For one, experts have only recently begun to seriously track youth doping. Another reason is because testing is expensive. In Florida, experts say testing would cost $150 per athlete. That would add up to $42 million per year to test every high school athlete.

Still, some states are pushing for tougher PED policies. The result could be more drug testing. The push also focuses on adults. Coaches and parents are in a position of influence. New laws could put stricter punishments on adults who allow PED use. Punishment is only half of the solution, though. Education is also important to prevent doping before it starts.

The efforts to educate youth athletes about the dangers of PEDs are widespread. Several organizations teach athletes and sports organizations about the dangers of doping. Among the leaders in this effort is Don Hooton, Taylor's dad. He created the Taylor Hooton Foundation. It works to educate teens and others about the dangers of steroid use.

Don Hooton wants schools to teach kids about the dangers of anabolic steroids and other PEDs. However, no laws about PED use specifically among youths have been passed through 2013. Don Hooton is working to change that.

BALANCED DIET

Some kids feel that PEDs are the best way to bulk up and build muscles. Doctors disagree. PEDs have negative side effects that can cause life-long health issues or even death. A better solution, says Dr. Linn Goldberg, is a balanced diet. Goldberg works at Oregon Health and Science University in Portland. He also helped develop two programs that teach high school kids about doping and nutrition. One program is called Athletes Training and Learning to Avoid Steroids (ATLAS). The other is Athletes Targeting Healthy Exercise and Nutrition Alternatives (ATHENA). Goldberg said kids should focus on eating protein-rich food and a healthy breakfast. He also warned against using supplements without consulting with a doctor or nutritionist first. "You don't know what's in them," he said.

Don Hooton, president of the Taylor Hooton ▲
Foundation, speaks against anabolic steroid use
at a press conference in 2013.

In the meantime, Hooton and others have turned to professional athletes for help. Dr. David Marks works at a testosterone replacement therapy clinic. He said, "If those [professional sports stars] can stand up and really educate the youth, I think that will have more impact than some government bureaucrat or doctor because, let's face it, kids look up to those guys."

CHAPTER 4

Cyclist Floyd Landis admitted to using PEDs to help him win the 2006 Tour de France. ▶

LOSING IT ALL

In professional sports, athletic success often leads to lifestyle changes. A successful athlete might earn lots of money, become famous, and create new business partnerships. For some athletes, these perks are appealing enough to justify the risks of using PEDs.

PEDs might help athletes perform better in competition. But athletes who use PEDs are taking a major risk. And the risks go far beyond the serious health problems that come with PEDs. An athlete caught or even suspected of doping can be suspended. A suspended athlete does not earn a paycheck. In addition, public opinion about an athlete often declines when the athlete is caught doping. Some fans no longer cheer

for the athlete. Companies cancel endorsement contracts. This can affect the athlete's financial security well beyond his or her playing career. The loss of fame and fortune can also be traumatizing.

MARION JONES

Marion Jones was the greatest female sprinter of her time. The American won three gold medals and two bronze medals at the 2000 Olympic Games. She was the fastest woman in the world. Her athletic success helped her become famous. But she was doping. Jones had used illegal PEDs to help her run faster. Federal agents asked Jones if she was doping. She said no. Lying to federal agents is a crime. In 2007, she admitted she had lied. Jones had to return her Olympic medals. She also went to prison for six months. "It is with a great amount of shame that I stand before you and tell you that I have betrayed your trust," Jones said before going to jail. "I have let my country down and I have let myself down."

Floyd Landis found out the hard way what doping can do to a sports career. The cyclist from Farmersville, Pennsylvania, was a rising star in his sport. From 2002 to 2004, he was Lance Armstrong's teammate. Landis played a key role in helping Armstrong win the Tour de France all three years.

In 2006, Landis was ready to make a run. Armstrong had retired after the 2005 Tour. Landis was now the star of his own team. However, a painful hip injury struck Landis. Then a terrible ride in the sixteenth stage appeared to end his hopes of a title. But Landis burst through the seventeenth stage with an inspired ride. In one stage he went from being 8 minutes, 8 seconds back to just 30 seconds behind. Before long, Landis was in the lead. That is where he remained when the more than 2,270-mile (3,653-km) race was finished.

Afterward, the race director called Landis's race "the best performance in the modern history of the Tour." Until suddenly it was not.

A urine sample taken after the seventeenth stage showed Landis
had higher-than-allowed levels of testosterone. That usually occurs
when somebody has taken anabolic steroids. Then another urine sample
confirmed the high testosterone.

Landis denied the doping charges. He said the testosterone levels
were natural. But the damage had already begun. The Tour de France
said it no longer considered Landis champion. The Phonak cycling team
fired Landis. Those in the cycling community and the media were quick to
condemn the champion.

STRAIGHT TO THE SOURCE

In 2013, Milwaukee Brewers outfielder Ryan Braun admitted to using banned PEDs during his MVP season in 2011. Afterward, he released a statement apologizing for his actions. As part of the statement, he explained what happened:

> During the latter part of the 2011 season, I was dealing with a nagging injury and I turned to products for a short period of time that I shouldn't have used. The products were a cream and a lozenge, which I was told could help expedite my rehabilitation. It was a huge mistake for which I am deeply ashamed and I compounded the situation by not admitting my mistakes immediately.

> Source: The Associated Press. "Ryan Braun Statement Text." NBC Sports. NBC Universal, 22 Aug. 2013. Web. 7 Sept. 2013.

Take a Stand

Ryan Braun is not the only athlete who said he used PEDs to help recover from an injury. Some people believe that is a reasonable excuse for using PEDs. Do you think using banned PEDs for any reason is acceptable? Write 200 words explaining your view.

In September 2007, the drug tests were upheld. Landis was officially stripped of his Tour de France title. He also was banned from competitive cycling for two years. Landis now had a different place in Tour de France history. In the 105 years of the event, no other winner had lost his title due to doping.

Landis had fallen from grace before he could even celebrate his victory. But for years after the positive test, he never gave up his fight. Landis wanted to prove he was innocent. He reportedly spent $2 million trying to clear his name. Then finally, in 2010, he had a change of heart. Landis admitted that he had used anabolic steroids for most of his professional career.

"I don't feel guilty at all about having doped," Landis said. "I did what I did because that's what we [cyclists] did . . . and that was a decision I had to make to make the next step. My choices were, do it and see if I can win, or don't do it and I tell people I just don't want to [dope], and I decided to do it."

Landis's legacy was officially tarnished. He tried to rebuild his cycling career after his ban was complete. But he never came close to the success he had earlier in his career. Landis had lost nearly everything—his life savings, his reputation, his career. Eventually he faded out of the public eye, disillusioned with the sport he once loved.

▲ Oakland Athletics sluggers Jose Canseco, *right*, and Mark McGwire later admitted to using PEDs.

REDEMPTION

Using PEDs is a choice. If an athlete is caught using PEDs, he or she can never erase that. The athlete might come back to the sport and compete cleanly. But the stigma of doping always remains.

Still, some athletes attempt to rehabilitate their reputations. One way to do that is by trying to help clean up their sports. When Landis admitted he had used PEDs, he also accused several other riders of doping. One of those he accused was Armstrong. "I don't want to be part of the problem anymore," Landis said.

Armstrong and others were quick to fight back. They attacked Landis as a cheater who could not be trusted. Many fans sided with Armstrong, who had never tested positive. The perception of Landis changed in 2012 and 2013. That is when Armstrong and many others Landis accused admitted to doping. Many credit Landis's accusations with giving momentum to the efforts to catch Armstrong and others.

"Floyd was the first guy to come out," bike race promoter Dieter Drake said. "Some might view that as a bad PR move, but I think he'll end up being on the right side of history."

Similar stories exist in other sports. Jose Canseco was one of baseball's best sluggers during the 1980s and 1990s. Then, in 2005, he released a book titled *Juiced: Wild Times, Rampant 'Roids, Smash Hits, and How Baseball Got Big*. In the book, Canseco admitted to using PEDs to become a top power hitter. He also wrote of a massive doping culture within baseball. Canseco accused several big stars of also using PEDs.

At first, Canseco was ridiculed. Some people did not want to believe his claims. Others accused Canseco of making wild claims to help sell copies of the book. People also noted that some of the details were sloppy. However, many of Canseco's claims were later found to be true.

Some even credit his book with helping kick-start baseball's efforts to combat doping.

NEVER THE SAME

Disgraced athletes have played a major role in cleaning up their sports. Their athletic legacies can never fully be recovered, though. Canadian sprinter Ben Johnson has experienced that. He was at the focus of one of the highest-profile doping violations ever.

Johnson set the 100-meter dash world record of 9.83 seconds in 1987. He was the favorite heading into the 1988 Olympic Games in Seoul, South Korea. And Johnson lived up to the hype. The race proved to be one of the fastest ever. Four runners broke the 10-second barrier. Johnson, however, took any drama out of the race. He blew US superstar Carl Lewis and the other runners away. Johnson powered to a new world record at 9.79 seconds. Lewis was second at 9.92. In a 100-meter sprint, that is a wide margin.

However, a urine sample taken from Johnson after the race found traces of a banned anabolic steroid. Within 24 hours of winning, he had given back his gold medal. His record was wiped away. It is estimated that he lost approximately $3 million in potential commercial earnings.

PEDs were common in track and field at the time. Eventually, six of the eight runners in that race tested positive or were linked to PEDs in some way. It has been called the "dirtiest race in history." Johnson stood by his decision. "I said to myself, 'Why should I do this clean when everyone

Canadian sprinter Ben Johnson surges ahead ▲
of his opponents during the 1988 Olympic
100-meter dash final.

else is cheating? That's unfair,'" he said. But for generations that followed, Johnson remained the face of the scandal.

Johnson later tried to change his image. He said he wants young athletes to know they do not have to cheat to run their fastest. But his legacy remains that of a cheater. In 2013, Johnson returned to Seoul for the twenty-fifth anniversary of that race.

"I was nailed on a cross," he said, "and 25 years later I'm still being punished."

PREVENTION AND PUNISHMENT

D oping has existed as long as people have been competing in sports. But as sports became more sophisticated, more intricate doping methods followed. As PED use has increased, officials have worked to find ways to catch users.

The battle against doping began in earnest in 1928. That is when the international governing body for track and field introduced the first PED ban. Steroid tests became common during the 1960s and 1970s. The Olympics began testing for PEDs in 1968 and for anabolic steroids in 1976. But these efforts left much to be desired. High-profile doping efforts were not punished. East Germany had a systematic doping scheme during the

1970s. PEDs helped the country dominate at the Olympic Games during that era. The depth of the doping program was not revealed until years later. In 1988, sprinter Ben Johnson tested positive for anabolic steroids. Fans were stunned. Yet even that incident did not lead to immediate action.

Important steps to combat doping finally occurred in November 1999. One year earlier, a massive doping scandal was uncovered at the Tour de France. Organizers of all sports were embarrassed. They realized their attempts to keep their sports clean were failing. A big reason for that was inconsistency. Each sport approached PED usage differently. So the International Olympic Committee held a meeting to improve the situation. And in November 1999, WADA was founded.

WADA is an independent agency. Its purpose is to lead a unified, global effort to prevent doping. This effort includes research into PEDs and new tests. WADA also sets lab standards and testing procedures, in addition to maintaining a list of banned substances. The list is included in the World

STEPPED UP EFFORTS

Cycling, long known for rampant doping, is becoming a leader in doping prevention. Public pressure has forced cycling to improve its anti-doping efforts. The UCI created an anti-doping program. Its program is considered one of the best in the world by WADA. Among the highlights is an improved testing model. Cyclists' blood and urine are tested for PEDs in and out of competition. In addition, all cyclists have a biological passport. This keeps track of the athletes' test results and other information. The passport helps give a long-term understanding of an athlete's body. That makes it easier to detect when PEDs are changing somebody's natural chemistry. In addition, athletes must let anti-doping officials know their whereabouts at all times. That is so the athletes can always be subject to testing.

Anti-Doping Code. Every sport in the Olympics and Paralympics abides by WADA's regulations at major events.

Outside major events, doping control falls to the individual countries and sports bodies. USADA was founded in 2000. It manages drug testing in the United States. USADA is also involved in research and education. All of the national governing bodies under the US Olympic Committee follow USADA's and WADA's policies. However, USADA and WADA do not have oversight of the major professional sports leagues. Leagues such as the NFL and MLB each set their own anti-doping policies.

ANTI-DOPING POLICIES

The push to clean up professional sports in the United States began in earnest around 2003. PEDs in US sports were not new. But the power numbers in baseball put the issue to the forefront. Then the Bay Area Laboratory Co-Operative (BALCO) scandal hit. The US government found that BALCO had distributed PEDs to several athletes. Among them were high-profile track-and-field stars. The most attention went to the baseball players linked to BALCO, such as Barry Bonds.

Baseball had no official anti-doping policy at the time. Finally, the sport had to take action. MLB implemented its first anti-doping policy in 2003. The policy was expanded in 2004 and toughened in 2005. Still, many doping experts believed the measures were too weak. With changes still in 2011 and again in 2013, however, MLB has become a leader among US sports.

▲ New York Yankees star Alex Rodriguez admitted to using PEDs early in his career, before MLB's anti-doping policy.

Baseball now tests for 70 kinds of steroids and 50 types of stimulants. All major league players can now be tested. The managers, coaches, and select locker room employees can also be tested. Testing can be done at any time without notice. Any player who tests positive for a banned PED is suspended for 50 games. A second positive test results in a 100-game suspension. A third positive test bans the player from baseball for life. These punishments are more severe than those in other US sports leagues.

The NFL first introduced a PED policy in 1987. Today, NFL players can be tested during the entire season. Every player gets tested at least once a year. The first positive test results in a four-game suspension. A player testing positive twice receives an eight-game suspension. The third time, it's for an entire season. The NFL has generally received less scrutiny than MLB for its doping policies. As such, some criticize the NFL as being too weak.

The other major US sports leagues have drug testing. Players who test positive receive suspensions. Four positive tests result in banishment from the National Basketball Association (NBA). It only takes three positive tests to be banned from the National Hockey League (NHL). The National Collegiate Athletic Association (NCAA) bans an athlete from playing college sports after two positive tests. However, the levels of testing in each sport differ. For example, the NBA was criticized for not conducting blood testing as of 2013. Blood testing identifies PEDs better than urine testing.

Much progress has been made to combat doping in the major US professional sports. However, the international standards set by WADA tend to be stricter. Athletes competing in Olympic sports can be tested at any time during the year. One failed drug test results in a two-year ban from competition. A second failed drug test is a lifetime ban.

AGAINST THE LAW

Anabolic steroid use was rampant in sports during the 1980s. So in 1991, the US government passed a law that labeled anabolic steroids a controlled substance. That essentially meant that owning, creating, or selling anabolic steroids without government permission was illegal. A person caught owning anabolic steroids can be given a fine and sent to prison for a year. Somebody caught selling or transporting anabolic steroids can get up to five years in prison and a $250,000 fine. Punishments can be worse if somebody has had a previous drug offense. In 2004, President George W. Bush signed the Anabolic Steroid Control Act. Among other things, the bill added steroid precursors and andro to the list of controlled substances. Not all PEDs are controlled substances, though. Anything prescribed by a doctor or available over the counter without restrictions is legal.

EDUCATION

Testing and punishment are only part of the battle to prevent doping. Education is the other big part. Several organizations and sports leagues have stepped up their efforts on education. The goal is to convince athletes never to use PEDs in the first place.

This education is particularly important among youth athletes. These athletes do not have the same resources or support structures as professionals. Many young people feel they are invincible. They also face unique health risks. And the negative effects from PEDs could impact their entire lives.

The Taylor Hooton Foundation, ATLAS, and ATHENA are among the groups leading the efforts to educate youth athletes. ATLAS and ATHENA are geared specifically toward high school athletes. Their programs involve a coach and a fellow student-athlete leading sessions with small groups. Usually these sessions take place during a regular practice. In small groups, the athletes learn about proper nutrition and sports training techniques. The students also discuss the negative effects of PEDs, supplements, and other drugs. A partnership with the NFL has helped expand the programs.

The Taylor Hooton Foundation is more wide ranging. Its goal is ultimately to combat doping among youth athletes. A major way it does that is through education. The foundation leads educational programs throughout the United States. It also has online programs on its Web site. In addition, the foundation works with legislators to help push for new laws. The Taylor Hooton Foundation has also partnered with other organizations to help expand its efforts. Among the foundation's partners are MLB, the NFL, and the NHL.

WADA and USADA have education programs as well. They aim to educate both amateur and professional athletes about the risks of anabolic steroids. In addition, these organizations emphasize how to avoid accidentally doping. Doping and doping prevention have become highly specialized. So many substances are banned that it can be hard to keep track.

WADA and other organizations have resources for athletes. These resources let the athletes know what substances are banned. The resources also educate the athletes about their rights and about drug testing. Sports organizations do not accept excuses. They expect athletes to know the rules and know what they are putting into their bodies.

THE NATIONAL CENTER FOR DRUG FREE SPORT

The National Center for Drug Free Sport is dedicated to preventing drug abuse in athletics. This organization does the drug testing for organizations such as the NCAA, the NFL, and minor league baseball. In addition, the organization has a hotline and a Web site for athletes. The athletes can use these resources to get answers to questions on anabolic steroids and dietary supplements. The organization also does customized education programs for groups.

But WADA and other organizations want to make sure athletes know how to find those resources.

The battle to prevent doping in sports is in full swing. However, doping is more sophisticated than ever. Scientists are working to find new PEDs that cannot be detected. And athletes are willing to take them. Organizations like WADA are hoping that through education, testing, and punishment, it can stay ahead of the dopers and make sports clean.

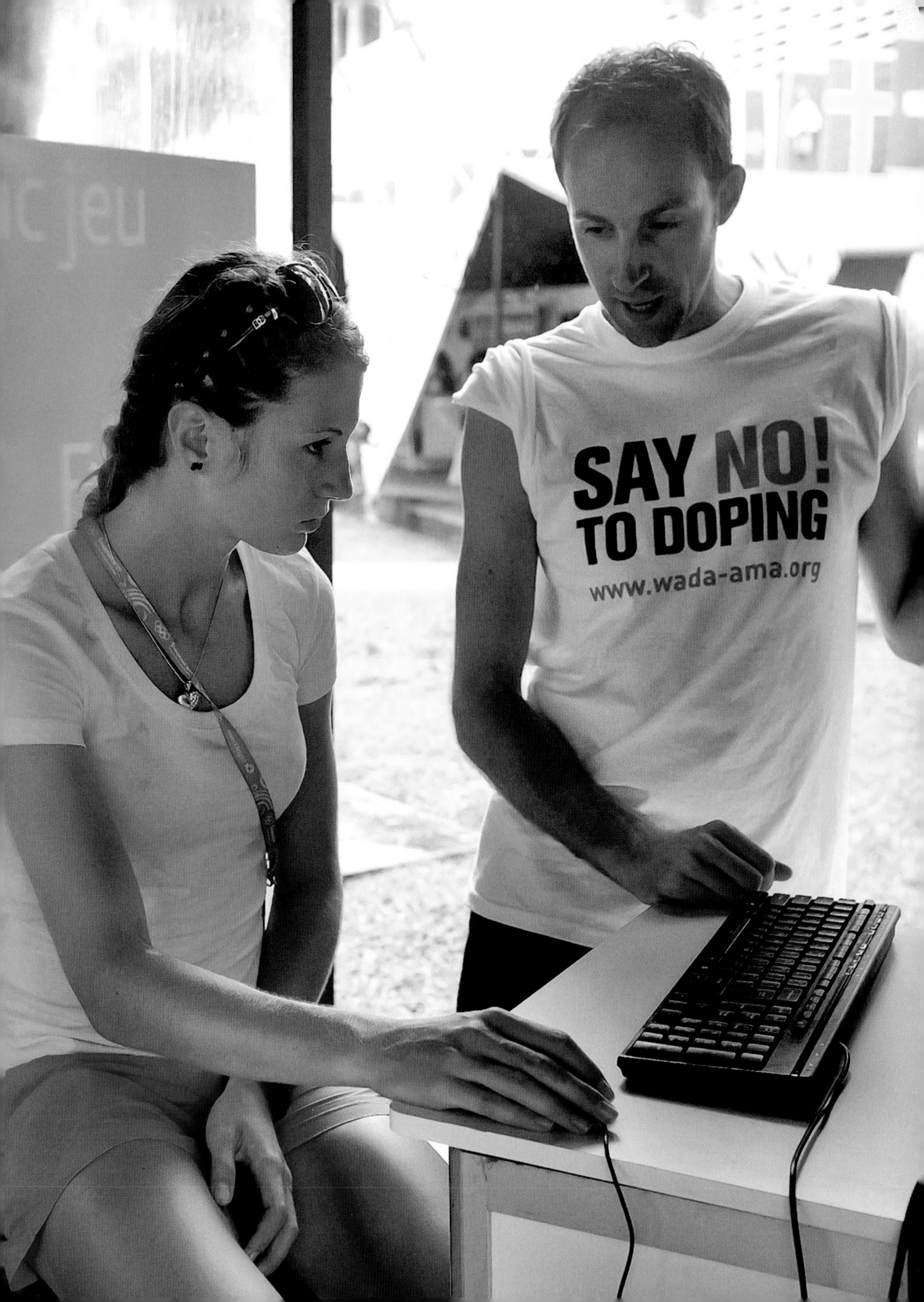
SAY NO!
TO DOPING
www.wada-ama.org

Why Do I Care?

You might not use PEDs. Maybe you don't know anybody who does. But sports officials and doctors are increasingly concerned about PEDs. List five reasons why people are concerned about PEDs. Then write a paragraph explaining why PEDs are an issue for everybody, not just those directly involved.

You Are There

Put yourself in the shoes of a sprinter at the 1988 Olympic Games. You are one of the fastest sprinters in the world. But many of your competitors are using PEDs. Taking PEDs yourself might give you a better chance at winning a medal. What would you do? Write a short blog entry explaining whether or not you would have used PEDs.

Take a Stand

Sports organizations have taken a stand against PEDs. But some people believe this is a losing battle. They think PEDs should be open to all adult athletes to level the playing field. What do you think? Should all adult athletes be allowed to use PEDs? Or should sports officials focus on the negative health effects and continue their fight against doping in sports?

amphetamines

Drugs that stimulate one's nervous system. Amphetamines are legal with a doctor's prescription.

anabolic steroids

Man-made testosterone drugs that promote tissue growth, among other things.

doping

A term used to describe the use of PEDs to improve athletic performance.

endorsements

When companies pay famous people to promote the companies, their products, or both.

menstruation

A process that occurs within the female sex organs each month to prepare females for pregnancy.

stimulants

Substances that help improve an athlete's performance by improving focus, energy, and how hard he or she plays. Amphetamines and caffeine are forms of stimulants.

synthetic

Artificial or man-made.

FOR MORE INFORMATION

SELECTED BIBLIOGRAPHY

Albergotti, Reed, and Vanessa O'Connell. "Lance Armstrong Admits to Doping, 'One Big Lie.'" *The Wall Street Journal*. Dow Jones & Company, 18 Jan. 2013. Web. 4 Oct. 2013.

Alzado, Lyle. "I'm Sick and I'm Scared." *SI Vault*. Time Inc., 8 July 1991. Web. 4 Oct. 2013.

Canseco, Jose. *Juiced: Wild Times, Rampant 'Roids, Smash Hits and How Baseball Got Big*. New York: Regan, 2005. Print.

Fainaru-Wada, Mark, and Lance Williams. *Game of Shadows*. New York: Gotham, 2006. Print.

Longman, Jere. "Drugs in Sports; An Athlete's Dangerous Experiment." *New York Times*. The New York Times Company, 26 Nov. 2003. Web. 4 Oct. 2013.

FURTHER READINGS

Cooper, Chris. *Run, Swim, Throw, Cheat: The Science Behind Drugs in Sport*. Oxford, UK: Oxford U.P., 2012. Print.

Fretland VanVoorst, Jennifer. *Performance-Enhancing Risks: The Science of Steroids*. Mankato, MN: Compass Point, 2010. Print.

Roleff, Tamara L. Ed. *Performance-Enhancing Drugs*. Detroit, MI: Greenhaven, 2010. Print.

WEB SITES

To learn more about performance-enhancing drugs in sports, visit ABDO Publishing Company online at **www.abdopublishing.com**. Web sites about performance-enhancing drugs in sports are featured on our Book Links page. These links are routinely monitored and updated to provide the most current information available.

PLACES TO VISIT

Newport Sports Museum
100 Newport Center Drive #100
Newport Beach, CA 92660
949-721-9333
www.newportsportsmuseum.org
This museum aims to promote healthy lifestyles through its memorabilia and partnerships with famous athletes. In addition, the museum has free programs meant to help instill confidence in children and teens.

US Olympic Training Center
1 Olympic Plaza
Colorado Springs, CO 80909
719-866-4618
www.teamusa.org
The Colorado Springs Olympic Training Center contains top-end training facilities for US Olympic hopefuls. Many athletes live and train here year-round. A 45-minute tour is available to the public.

INDEX

ABOUT THE AUTHOR

Tony Khing has been in professional sports for more than 20 years. He has been a manager of media relations, Internet content, and communications for teams in each of the four major professional sports. He has written and edited books on the San Francisco Giants, San Jose Sharks, and the World Series. He graduated from San Francisco State University with a bachelor degree in radio/television and a minor in journalism.